Activities

Each topic in this book comes with a simple craft activity or yummy recipe for you to enjoy at home. Here are some helpful tips to get you started.

Materials

It's useful to have some materials ready such as cereal and tissue boxes, thicker card and card tubes for when you feel creative.

Several activities in this book use recycled items and perhaps you could think of some more ideas.

Templates

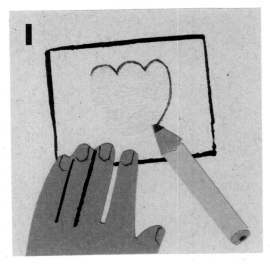

1 Place a piece of tracing paper over the template. Hold steady and draw around the shape.

2 Turn the tracing paper over and scribble over the lines with a soft pencil.

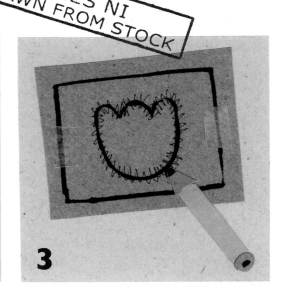

3 Turn over again and tape onto paper or card. Retrace firmly over the original lines. Remove tracing paper.

TIP You can use greaseproof paper instead of tracing paper.

Birds

peregrine falcon

baby little owls

swallow

swift

green woodpecker

Birds live all round the world, from freezing Antarctica to huge, humid cities. Wherever we are, we can see them flying in the skies and hear them singing to one another. Some birds stay in one place. Some migrate (move) thousands of miles to live in warmer or colder regions for part of the year. And some birds don't fly at all.

All birds are covered in feathers, have a beak and lay eggs. Most birds lay their eggs in nests where the parent birds keep the eggs warm until the baby birds hatch out.

starling

wren

4

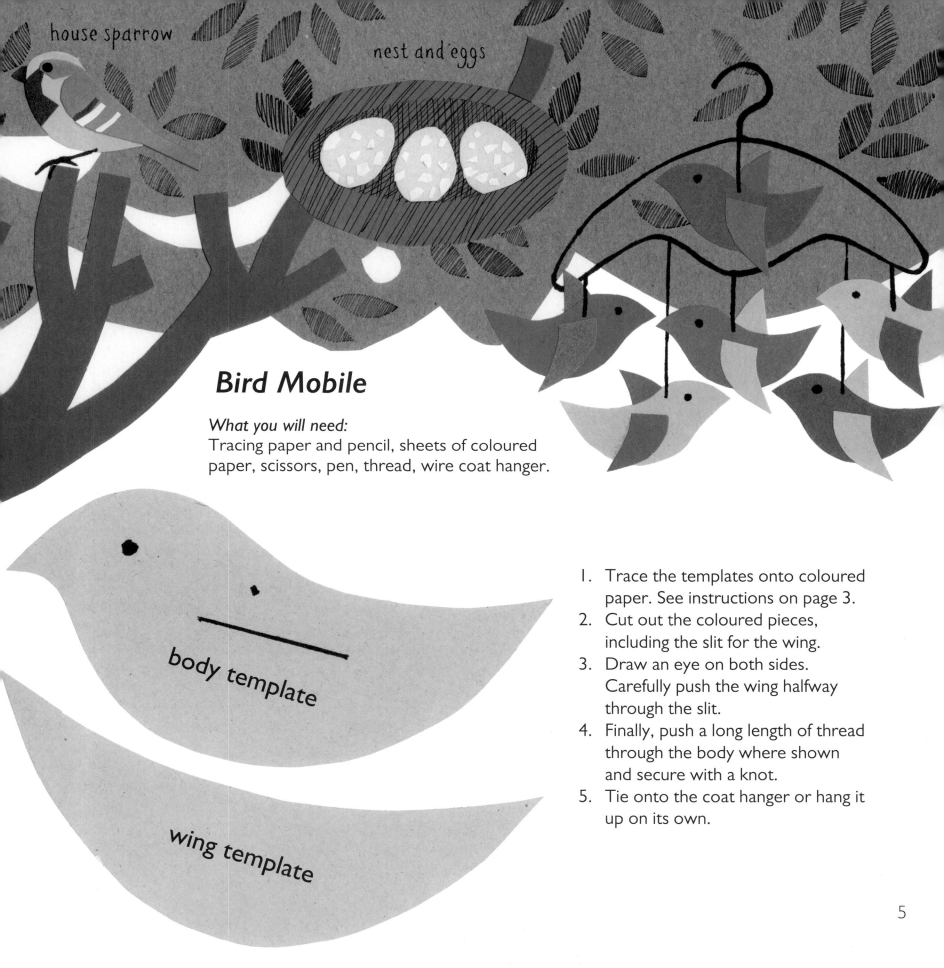

house sparrow

nest and eggs

Bird Mobile

What you will need:
Tracing paper and pencil, sheets of coloured paper, scissors, pen, thread, wire coat hanger.

body template

wing template

1. Trace the templates onto coloured paper. See instructions on page 3.
2. Cut out the coloured pieces, including the slit for the wing.
3. Draw an eye on both sides. Carefully push the wing halfway through the slit.
4. Finally, push a long length of thread through the body where shown and secure with a knot.
5. Tie onto the coat hanger or hang it up on its own.

Wild Flowers

bindweed

white campion

Wild flowers grow naturally in every part of the world, from sandy deserts to the tops of mountains. In the past, people picked them for food, colour dyes, perfumes and even medicinal uses. Today, cities and towns are much bigger so wild flowers have less space. They are now rarer and we mustn't pick them.

The name dandelion comes from the French for lion's tooth – dent de lion – inspired by the shape of the leaves. People used to cure illnesses with the leaves but now they eat them in salads or make wine with them.

bluebell

primrose

snail

daisy

violet

6

Floral Crown

What you will need:

Thin yellow or gold card 5 cm (2 in) wide and 56 cm (22 in) long, coloured tissue paper, green paper, sticky tape and scissors.

1. Cut the tissue paper into circles using the template.
2. Push the point of the scissors through the card band in the middle at 2.5-cm (1-in) intervals all the way round.
3. Place two tissue circles together and push the point through the hole, securing at the back of the band with tape. Fluff out the flower. Carry on until all the holes are filled. (See picture.)
4. Cut out some small, green paper leaves using the leaf template (see page 3) and tape amongst the flowers.
5. Join the band to fit your head and finish with long tissue paper streamers taped inside by the back join.

flower template

see page 3 for instructions

leaf template

dandelion

TIP You will need two tissue paper circles for every flower.

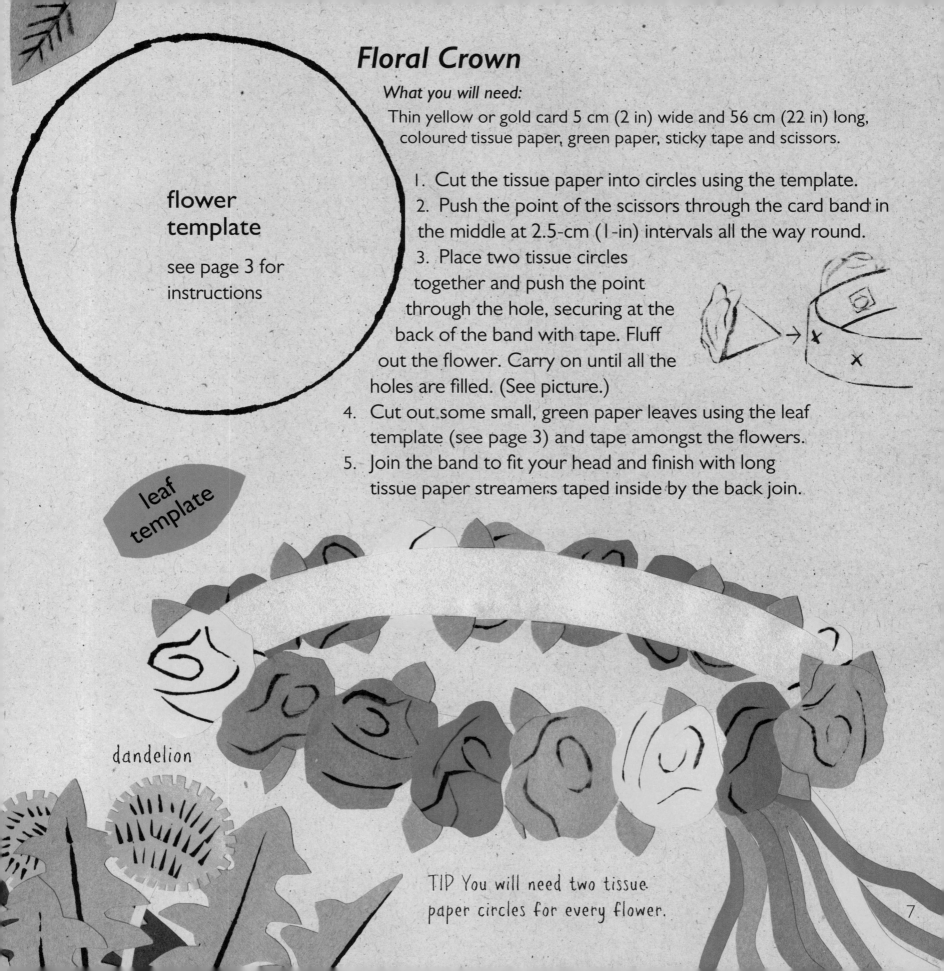

7

ants

bee

Insects

fly

ladybirds

There are over one million different types of insect. Insects all have six legs and two feelers. Their eyes are made up of lots of tiny lenses. They mostly live alone but some such as bees and ants live in large, organised groups. There are insects that destroy things such as food, wood or wool. Others, like mosquitoes, spread diseases. But many insects are our friends. Bees make honey and keep flowers alive by collecting and carrying pollen. Silkworms make silk. Ladybirds stop smaller insects from eating our plants by eating them!

dragonfly

wasp

cinnabar moth caterpillar

red admiral butterfly

small heath butterfly

beetle

grasshopper

oak eggar
moth

common blue
butterfly

butterfly template

Fluttering Butterfly

What you will need:
Thin coloured papers, tracing paper and pencil,
glue and sticky tape, scissors.

1. Trace the butterfly template onto coloured
   paper (see instructions on page 3) and cut out.
2. Decorate with glued shapes of coloured paper.
3. Fold the wings up along the sides of the body.

4. Cut a paper strip measuring 2.5 cm (1 in) wide
   and 7 cm (3 in) long and tape it to the middle of
   the underside of the body.
5. Tape the strip to fit around
   your forefinger.
6. Wave your finger to flutter!

9

Twigs

goldfinch

The largest part of a tree is the trunk. It is covered in bark and usually upright. Small branches grow out in different directions from the trunk. Then, from these branches, even smaller twigs grow. These twigs are where leaves, buds, flowers and fruit form.

When twigs fall off the trees, birds such as pigeons, crows, eagles and squirrels pick them up and use them to build their nests.

American goldfinch

European goldfinch

blackbird

10

Stars and Snowflakes

What you will need:
Twigs (choose dry fallen ones and avoid ones with thorns), string, wool or raffia, thin wire, strong scissors or secateurs (adults only!), paints and brush.

TIP Try out your own designs using different colours, decorations and sizes.

SNOWFLAKE

1. Cut three twigs of the same width to the same length.
2. Glue two smaller twigs near the end of each of these three twigs. It doesn't matter if the angles aren't perfect.
3. Tie the twigs together in the centre with string, wool or raffia and hang up with a loop of string.
4. Paint the snowflake white if you like.

snowflake

STAR I

1. Cut five identical lengths of a similar type of twig.
2. Lay out as shown and tie together at the crossings with string, wool or raffia. You can secure them with thin wire first. Hang up from one of the points.

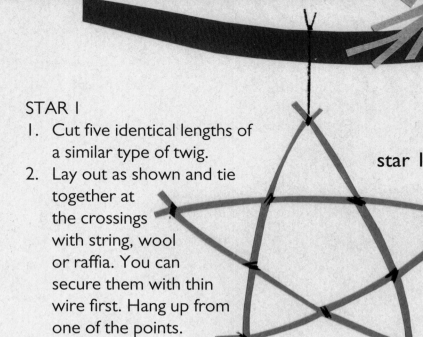

star I

STAR 2

Paint three identical twigs white or in stripes of white and red. Fix together in the centre with string, wool or raffia. Hang up with a loop of string.

STAR 3

Bunch together a few very thin twigs. Secure in the centre and at the ends with string, wool or raffia.

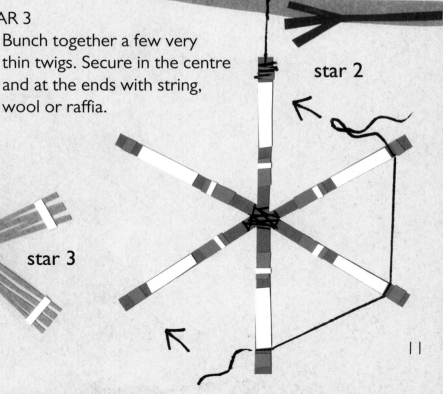

star 2

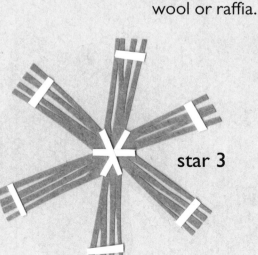

star 3

11

Leaves

oak

willow

hawthorn

spruce

horse chestnut

Trees are covered in leaves that help them to grow tall and stay strong. They grow from stems attached to the twigs on the tree. Much like the trees, leaves come in all sorts of shapes and sizes.

Evergreen trees stay green and keep their leaves all year round. Deciduous trees lose their leaves every year. They change colour and fall to the ground. In the spring, buds appear and new leaves start to grow.

elm leaf

autumn leaves

fir cone

walnut

elm

juniper

olive

ash

Leaf Printing

What you will need:
Leaves, water-based paints and brush, paper or card.

1. Just before you are going to use them, collect a number of different leaves. If you collect them too far in advance they will dry out and break.
2. Cover one side of the leaf in thick paint and place paint-down on the paper or card.
3. Press down carefully and remove. You can use it again, repaint it or paint another leaf.
4. Arrange in patterns and overlap if you like. Try different colours.
5. Leave the paper flat to dry. You can decorate cards, gift tags, wrapping paper or create a picture.

TIP If you paint on the back of the leaf the veins will show more.

Birds in Winter

great
tit

robin

red
squirrel

treecreeper

sparrow

As winter approaches, the weather gets
colder and it is harder for birds to find their
food. The insects, worms and seeds that birds
usually eat start to disappear. When this
happens, some types of bird gather in big
groups and fly together to warmer countries.
This is called migration. Other birds brave the
cold and stay in one place all year round. You
can help these birds by putting food out for them.

14

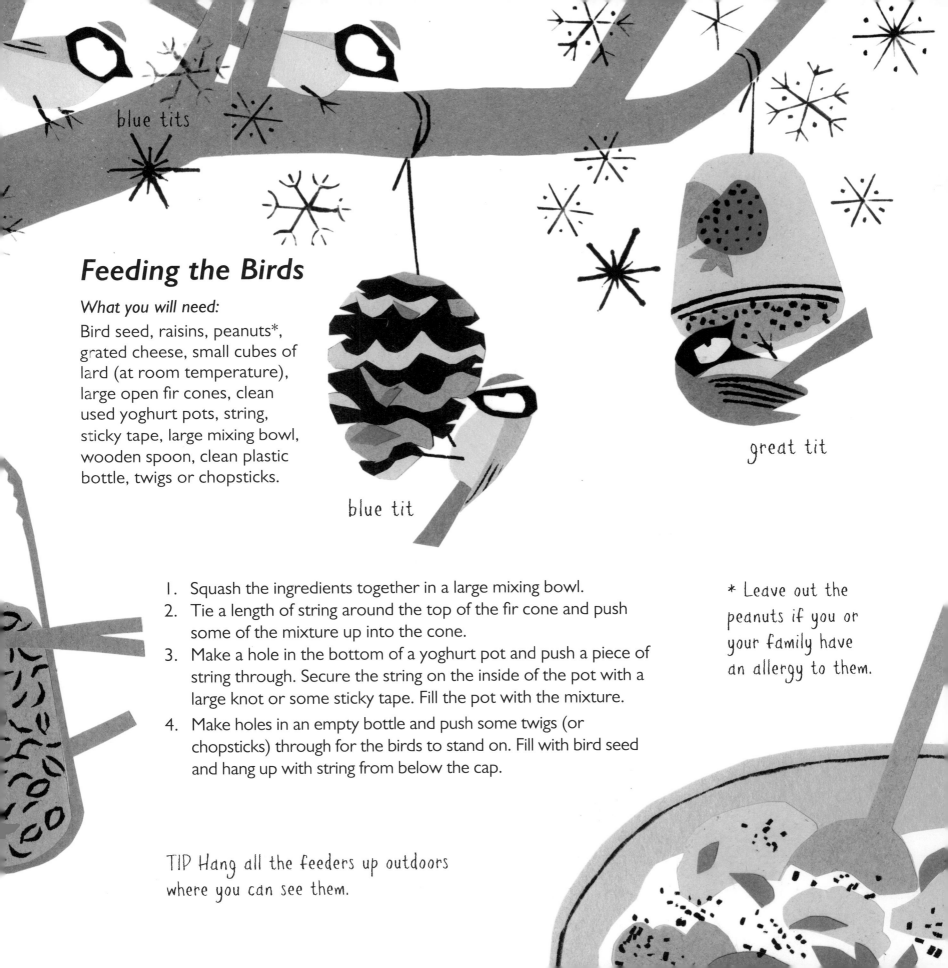

blue tits

Feeding the Birds

What you will need:

Bird seed, raisins, peanuts*, grated cheese, small cubes of lard (at room temperature), large open fir cones, clean used yoghurt pots, string, sticky tape, large mixing bowl, wooden spoon, clean plastic bottle, twigs or chopsticks.

blue tit

great tit

1. Squash the ingredients together in a large mixing bowl.
2. Tie a length of string around the top of the fir cone and push some of the mixture up into the cone.
3. Make a hole in the bottom of a yoghurt pot and push a piece of string through. Secure the string on the inside of the pot with a large knot or some sticky tape. Fill the pot with the mixture.
4. Make holes in an empty bottle and push some twigs (or chopsticks) through for the birds to stand on. Fill with bird seed and hang up with string from below the cap.

* Leave out the peanuts if you or your family have an allergy to them.

TIP Hang all the feeders up outdoors where you can see them.

Raccoons

Raccoons are the size of a small dog and they live mostly in North America. With a striking black mask around their eyes and a long, stripy tail, their fur is thick to keep them warm in the winter. They are good climbers, very clever and can use their front paws like hands.

It is not unusual to see raccoons living in towns and cities – they even eat food from dustbins! In captivity, they can live for 20 years but in the wild only up to three years.

Bear Mask

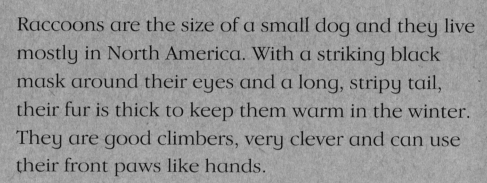

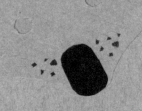

Use brown paper if you want to make a bear mask.

bat

raccoon
mask
template

Raccoon Mask

What you will need:
White paper or thin card, paints and brush
or coloured grey and black paper, pencil and
tracing paper, scissors, thin elastic.

1. Trace the mask (see instructions on
   page 3) including the outlines of the markings,
   eye holes and holes for the elastic.

2. Cut out and either paint the markings or
   use coloured paper to make them.
3. Tie one end of the elastic to one hole and
   the other to the second hole, to fit around
   your head.

TIP You could also use sticky tape to secure
the elastic at each side on the back.

Deer

red
deer

Deer come in lots of different sizes, from the
large moose to the tiny pudu.

All male deer have bony antlers that grow on their
heads. They shed their antlers every year and grow
new ones. A velvety skin covers antlers as they get
bigger then, when their antlers are fully grown, the deer
shed this skin. They use the antlers to fight each other!
The only female deer with antlers is the reindeer.

shed antler

fallow
deer

sika deer

18

Deer Family

What you will need:

Tracing paper and pencil, thin brown and green card, paints, brushes and felt-tip pens, scissors.

1. Trace the deer templates onto brown card (see instructions on page 3). You will need two sets of legs and one body for each adult deer.

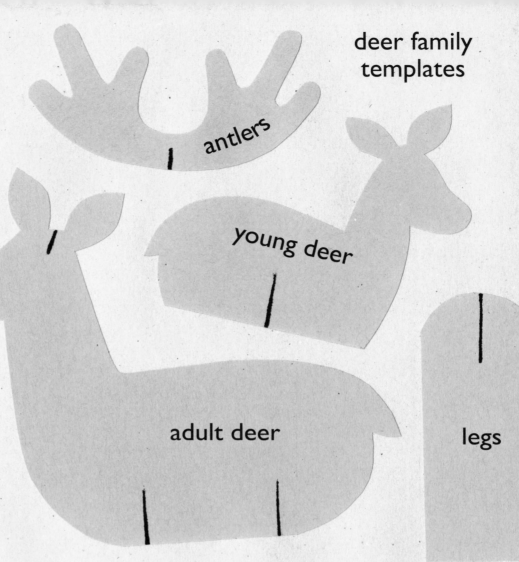

antlers

young deer

grass

adult deer

legs

2. Cut out the deer from the card.
3. Cut the slots marked. Only cut the slot on one of the adult deer's heads. This is where his antlers will go.
4. Add face details and spots on both sides.
5. Paint the antlers white on both sides. Leave to dry.
6. Slot together and stand up in a group.
7. Trace the grass template onto green card. Cut out the grass and slot in the young deer.

TIP You could cut out a base from green paper or card if you like.

19

Dreys and Warrens

squirrel's
drey

Wild animals need to make safe homes so they have somewhere warm to sleep, stay dry, bring up their young and even hide from their enemies.

Squirrels make their homes – called dreys – high up in the trees using twigs, leaves and grass. They make it comfortable with more grass and bits of tree bark.

Wild rabbits dig lots of tunnels underground to make one large warren that has nests, living areas and emergency exits. Whilst feeding on grass, wild rabbits stay close to the entrances.

rabbit
warren

Finger Puppets

What you will need:

Coloured felt, beads or small buttons, 10-cm (4-in) length of wool, needle and thread, scissors and glue, tracing paper, pencil and pins.

SQUIRREL, CHIPMUNK, MOUSE

1. Trace the template (see instructions on page 3). Pin the tracing paper onto the felt. Cut out the paper and felt together. Do this twice. Unpin and discard the paper.

2. Glue the black felt nose, stitch the black thread whiskers and sew on bead or button eyes on both felt pieces as shown.

3. Pin together and stitch around the body leaving the bottom open.

finger puppet templates

squirrel

chipmunk

Glue black felt stripes down the body and along the tail on both sides.

mouse

Knot one end of the wool and sew on at the bottom for the tail.

rabbit

See below for instructions.

RABBIT

Make the felt shapes as above. Sew the nose, mouth and whiskers in black thread on one piece only. Add some bead or button eyes. Pin the two pieces together and sew around the body. Glue the ears together. Add a white round felt tail at the back near the bottom.

TIP You can also make brightly coloured puppets.

21

Owls

long-eared owl

little owl

tawny owl

oak tree

Owls live all around the world. They are nocturnal, which means that they sleep during the day and are awake at night. As night falls, they start hunting for small animals such as mice, worms and large insects. They find their food using their extraordinary eyesight and hearing and can fly without making a sound. Owls have round faces and eyes that face forward – unlike other birds, whose eyes are on the sides of their heads.

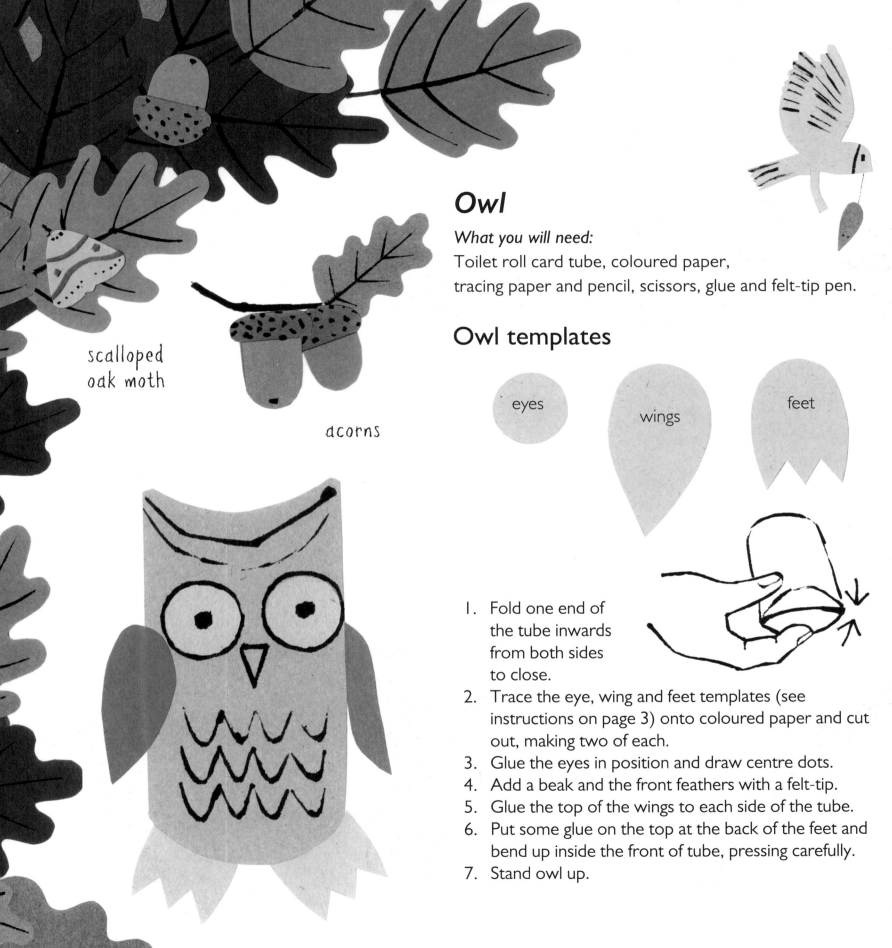

scalloped
oak moth

acorns

Owl

What you will need:
Toilet roll card tube, coloured paper,
tracing paper and pencil, scissors, glue and felt-tip pen.

Owl templates

eyes

wings

feet

1. Fold one end of the tube inwards from both sides to close.
2. Trace the eye, wing and feet templates (see instructions on page 3) onto coloured paper and cut out, making two of each.
3. Glue the eyes in position and draw centre dots.
4. Add a beak and the front feathers with a felt-tip.
5. Glue the top of the wings to each side of the tube.
6. Put some glue on the top at the back of the feet and bend up inside the front of tube, pressing carefully.
7. Stand owl up.

Fruit Trees

plums

pears

apples

Fruit grows on trees and bushes. Humans, animals, insects and birds all enjoy eating the fruit. In the spring, pretty flowers called blossom appear. The fruit then grows from the blossom during summer.

Pome fruits such as apples and pears have firm flesh and seeds in the middle. Stone fruits such as cherries, apricots and plums have soft flesh and a hard pit in the middle. These fruit trees often grow in fields called orchards. Citrus fruit such as oranges and lemons have thick skin and farmers plant them in groves.

apple blossom

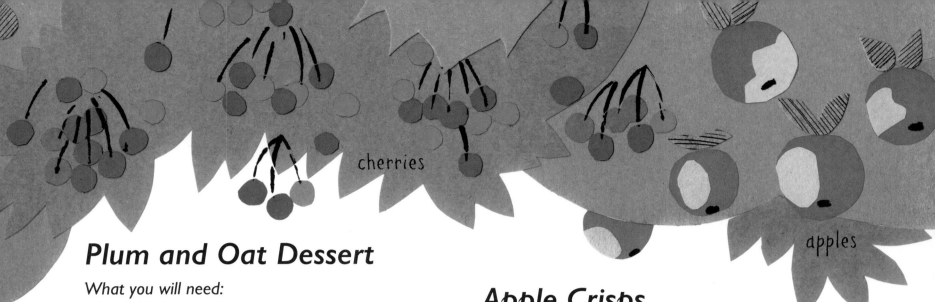

cherries

apples

Plum and Oat Dessert

What you will need:

450 g (1lb) plums, 1½ tsp cinnamon, 280 g (10 oz) organic wholemeal flour, 210 g (7½ oz) rolled oats, pinch of salt, 220 g (8oz) butter, 105 g (3½ oz) light brown soft sugar, baking tray, sharp knife, small pan, mixing bowl, wooden spoon.

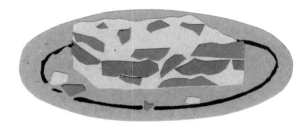

1. Lightly grease a deep 25 cm x 15 cm (10 in x 6 in) baking tray. Preheat the oven to 200° C (400° F) or Gas Mark 6 (ask an adult to help you).
2. Wash the plums and cut them in half, remove the stones, then cut into thin slices and place in a bowl with the cinnamon. Mix well.
3. Combine the flour, oats and salt in a mixing bowl.
4. Place the butter and sugar in a pan over a low heat and stir until melted.
5. Add to the flour mixture and stir well until a dough has formed.
6. Press half into the tray. Carefully cover with the plums then top with the rest of the dough, pressing down firmly.
7. Cook in the centre of the oven for 25-30 minutes.
8. Serve warm or cold with cream or yoghurt.

Apple Crisps

What you will need:

Two apples, cinnamon, sharp knife, baking trays and baking parchment.

1. Heat the oven to 150° C (300° F) or Gas Mark 2 (ask an adult to help you).
2. Line the baking trays with baking parchment.
3. Get an adult to core and cut the apples into very thin rings.
4. Place apple rings on the trays and sprinkle with cinnamon.
5. Cook for 45 minutes to an hour, turning halfway through, until the apples have dried out.
6. Cool and keep in an airtight container.

Freshwater Wildlife

Water covers more than two thirds of the planet and nearly all of it is salty like the sea. Inland lakes, canals, rivers and streams are not salty, the water is fresh. It is home to many plants and animals.

Reptiles, insects, fish and birds all live in fresh water and it is what humans, plants and animals need to live, too. If you sit for a while you will spot some of the creatures that live by, on and in the water.

kingfisher

water shrew

moorhen

mallard ducks

heron

minnows

frog

Sparkly Fish

What you will need:

Paper plates, coloured paper, scissors, sticky tape and glue, sequins and glitter, paints and brushes.

1. Cut one or two plates into fin and tail pieces.
2. Cut mouths from other plates and tape the fins and tails in position on the back.
3. Paint the front sides and leave to dry.
4. Cut out paper eyes and scales then glue in place.
5. Make your fish sparkle by gluing parts, pouring over glitter or sequins, and shaking off the excess onto a piece of scrap paper.

cut out fins   cut out tails   cut out mouths

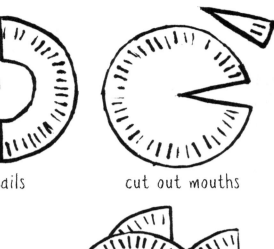

trout

Seashore

seagull

starfish

scallop

The seashore is where the land meets the sea. It constantly changes as the tide water moves up and down throughout the day. The water comes in twice a day. This is called high tide. It goes out twice a day, called low tide.

Seashores can be sandy, shingle (small pebbles) or rocky, or even mudflats or sand dunes. Many creatures, plants and seabirds feed and make their home on the seashore. Visiting the seashore is fun. We can explore rock pools, walk along sandy beaches and find pretty sea shells.

seaweed

hermit crab

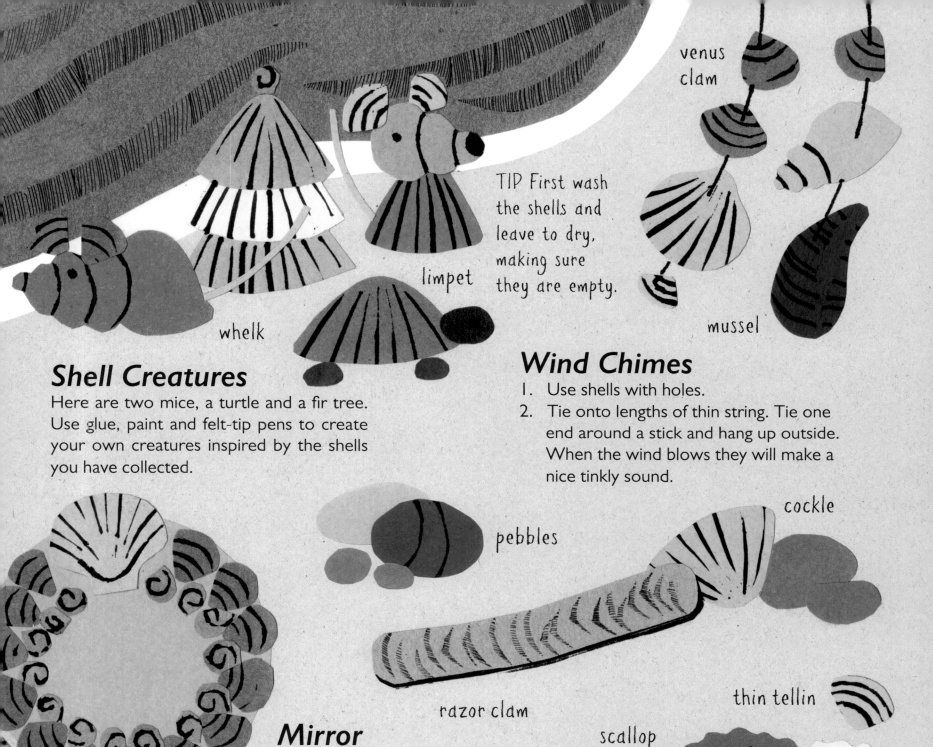

venus
clam

TIP First wash
the shells and
leave to dry,
making sure
they are empty.

limpet

mussel

whelk

Shell Creatures

Here are two mice, a turtle and a fir tree.
Use glue, paint and felt-tip pens to create
your own creatures inspired by the shells
you have collected.

Wind Chimes

1. Use shells with holes.
2. Tie onto lengths of thin string. Tie one
    end around a stick and hang up outside.
    When the wind blows they will make a
    nice tinkly sound.

cockle

pebbles

razor clam

thin tellin

scallop

Mirror

1. Collect enough shells to go around
    a mirror and lay out your pattern.
2. Glue a largish shell at centre top of the mirror.
3. Complete the circle with smaller shells.
    Put the glue on the mirror edge first.
    Press the shells firmly in position,
    keeping them close together.

winkle

29

Garden Flowers

daisies

forget-me-not

common blue butterfly

Flowers attract beautiful insects such as bees, which come to collect pollen from them, and butterflies, which feed on their nectar. Flowers need sunshine, good soil and water to grow.

Some flowers, called annuals, have bright and colourful petals that can last for up to one year. Perennial flowers last year after year but their petals only stay out for a short time. It is nice to have both types of flower in a garden or park.

cornflower

rose

daffodil

brimstone butterfly

aster

flower
templates

Vase of Flowers

What you will need:

An empty square tissue box, coloured papers and tape, scissors and glue, tracing paper and pencil, drinking straws, piece of newspaper, sticky tape.

1. Start by decorating the box with paper and tape to make a vase.
2. Scrunch up the newspaper and push it into the box. This will help the flowers stand up.
3. Trace the flowers and the leaves onto coloured paper (see instructions on page 3).
4. Cut lots of different coloured flowers and green leaves.
5. Glue round, coloured centres onto some flowers.
6. Tape flowers onto the tops of the straws, cutting some a little shorter, and add leaves.
7. Place in your 'vase'.

flower
templates

bee

tulip

leaf template

rudbeckia

Glossary

These unusual words help describe nature.
Some of them appear in the book. Here is what they mean.

ivy

wasp

annual – to do with one single year

antler – the bones that grow on the head of deer

captivity – keeping animals in cages

deciduous – trees that lose their leaves each year

drey – homes that squirrels make

evergreen – trees that keep their leaves all year round

freshwater – water that is not salty

grove – a field of citrus fruit trees

habitat – places where animals can live such as forests, towns, deserts

mammals – animals that have warm blood and do not lay eggs

medicinal – to do with medicine

migration – when a creature travels a long distance, usually in groups

native – was born in the place where it lives

nocturnal – active at night

orchard – a field of fruit trees

perennial – something that lasts for many years

pollen – a powder that helps flowers reproduce

pome fruit – fruits with flesh and seeds, like an apple

recycling – re-using rubbish like paper, glass

shed – to lose your skin on purpose

tropical – to do with 'the tropics' where the weather is hot and humid

urban – to do with towns and cities

warren – the maze of tunnels where rabbits live

Published by b small publishing ltd.

First published in paperback in 2017 by b small publishing ltd.

Nature Book   ISBN 978-1-911509-00-4   www.bsmall.co.uk

Text and illustrations © b small publishing 2016

Editorial: Jenny Jacoby & Susan Martineau Design: Louise Millar Production: Madeleine Ehm Publisher: Sam Hutchinson

1 2 3 4 5 6 7 8 9

orange tip butterfly

fly agaric fungus